20 SIMPLE SOUP MAKER RECIPES

by Dan Lee

-- All of the delicious soup recipes in this book are for a soup maker or machine with a 1.6 Ltr capacity, please adjust the recipe accordingly if your soup maker is larger or smaller --

-- notes pages are provided at the end of this recipe book for your convenience when making any recipe adjustments --

TOMATO & BASIL SOUP

INGREDIENTS

2x medium onions, chopped
3x garlic cloves, chopped (or 2 tbsp of garlic puree)
5x medium tomatoes, chopped
1x medium potato, chopped
1x large carrot, peeled and chopped
8x basil leaves, chopped
1x vegetable stock cube
Boiling water

INSTRUCTIONS

- Add all the ingredients **apart from the basil** to your soup maker.
- Add boiling water to top up your soup maker, ensure you do not go above the MAXIMUM or below the MINIMUM line.
- Put the lid on and select the smooth setting.
- At the end of the program, remove the lid and add the basil leaves. Use the blend setting for 30-60 seconds depending on preference.
- Serve and enjoy!

TOMATO & PEPPER SOUP

INGREDIENTS

1x medium onion, chopped
1x garlic clove, chopped (or 1 tbsp of garlic puree)
8x medium tomatoes, chopped
3x peppers, chopped
2x tbsp of tomato puree
Salt and pepper to taste
Boiling water

INSTRUCTIONS

- Add all the ingredients **apart from the salt and pepper** to your soup maker.
- Add boiling water to top up your soup maker, ensure you do not go above the MAXIMUM or below the MINIMUM line.
- Put the lid on and select the smooth setting.
- At the end of the program, add salt and pepper to taste. Use the blend setting for 30 seconds to mix
- Serve and enjoy!

TOMATO SOUP (CREAM OF)

INGREDIENTS

500ml Tomato Passata
400g tin of plum or chopped tomatoes
2x vegetable stock cube
100ml double cream
Skimmed milk to top up

INSTRUCTIONS

- Add all the ingredients to your soup maker.
- Add skimmed milk to top up your soup maker, ensure you do not go above the MAXIMUM or below the MINIMUM line.
- Put the lid on and select the smooth setting.
- Serve and enjoy!

BROCCOLI AND BLUE CHEESE SOUP

INGREDIENTS

1x large head of broccoli, chopped and stem removed
2x medium onions, chopped
2x large potatoes, chopped
2x vegetable stock cubes
200g of Stilton (or alternative blue cheese)
Ground black pepper
Boiling water

INSTRUCTIONS

- Add all of the ingredients **apart from the Stilton** to your soup maker.
- Add boiling water to top up your soup maker, ensure you do not go above the MAXIMUM or below the MINIMUM line.
- Put the lid on and select the smooth setting.
- When the program has finished, break the Stilton into smaller pieces and add to the soup maker, use the blend setting to reach desired consistency.
- Serve and enjoy!

BROCCOLI SOUP (SIMPLE)

INGREDIENTS

1x large head of broccoli, chopped and stem removed
2x medium onions, chopped
1x large potato, chopped
2x vegetable stock cubes
2x garlic cloves, chopped
Salt and pepper to taste
Boiling water

INSTRUCTIONS

- Add all of the ingredients to your soup maker.
- Add boiling water to top up your soup maker, ensure you do not go above the MAXIMUM or below the MINIMUM line.
- Put the lid on and select the smooth setting.
- Serve and enjoy!

BROCCOLI SOUP (SPICY)

INGREDIENTS

1x large head of broccoli, chopped and stem removed
1x small celeriac, chopped
5g fresh ginger
2x vegetable stock cubes
1x tsp ground cinnamon
1x tsp ground turmeric
Boiling water

INSTRUCTIONS

- Add all of the ingredients to your soup maker.
- Add boiling water to top up your soup maker, ensure you do not go above the MAXIMUM or below the MINIMUM line.
- Put the lid on and select the smooth setting.
- When the program has finished, allow to cool slightly and add further cinnamon or turmeric to taste
- Serve and enjoy!

PEA AND MINT SOUP

INGREDIENTS

2x medium onions, chopped
1x large potato, chopped
2x vegetable stock cubes
2x garlic cloves, chopped
400g frozen peas
10g fresh mint
Salt and pepper to taste
Boiling water
Optional cream cheese

INSTRUCTIONS

- Add all of the ingredients **apart from the mint (and cream cheese if using)** to your soup maker.
- Add boiling water to top up your soup maker, ensure you do not go above the MAXIMUM or below the MINIMUM line.
- Put the lid on and select the smooth setting.
- When the program has finished, finely chop the fresh mint and add to the soup maker, stir using a wooden spoon or use the blend setting for 5-10 seconds.
- Serve and enjoy!

Why not try adding a spoon of cream cheese to your bowl of Pea and Mint soup for a creamier dish!

PEA, MINT AND HAM SOUP

INGREDIENTS

2x medium onions, chopped
1x large potato, chopped
2x vegetable stock cubes
2x garlic cloves, chopped
300g frozen peas
200g cooked ham, chopped
10g fresh mint
Salt and pepper to taste
Boiling water

INSTRUCTIONS

- Add all of the ingredients **apart from the mint** to your soup maker.
- Add boiling water to top up your soup maker, ensure you do not go above the MAXIMUM or below the MINIMUM line.
- Put the lid on and select the smooth setting.
- When the program has finished, finely chop the fresh mint and add to the soup maker, stir using a wooden spoon or use the blend setting for 5-10 seconds.
- Serve and enjoy!

VEGETABLE SOUP (CREAM OF)

INGREDIENTS

2x medium onions, chopped
6x medium carrots, chopped
2x medium potatoes, chopped
1x swede, roughly chopped
2x vegetable stock cubes
100ml double cream
Skimmed milk to top up

INSTRUCTIONS

- Add all the ingredients to your soup maker.
- Add skimmed milk to top up your soup maker, ensure you do not go above the MAXIMUM or below the MINIMUM line.
- Put the lid on and select the smooth setting.
- Serve and enjoy!

VEGETABLE SOUP (SPICY)

INGREDIENTS

2x medium onions, chopped
6x medium carrots, chopped
2x medium potatoes, chopped
1x swede, roughly chopped
2x vegetable stock cubes
1x tsp salt
3x tsp ground black pepper
2x tsp chilli powder
1x tsp dried coriander
Boiling water

INSTRUCTIONS

- Add all the ingredients to your soup maker.
- Add boiling water to top up your soup maker, ensure you do not go above the MAXIMUM or below the MINIMUM line.
- Put the lid on and select the smooth setting.
- Serve and enjoy!

VEGETABLE SOUP (CHUNKY)

INGREDIENTS

2x medium onions, chopped
6x medium carrots, chopped
2x medium potatoes, chopped
1x swede, roughly chopped
2x vegetable stock cubes
1x tsp salt
3x tsp ground black pepper
Boiling water

INSTRUCTIONS

- Add all the ingredients to your soup maker.
- Add boiling water to top up your soup maker, ensure you do not go above the MAXIMUM or below the MINIMUM line.
- Put the lid on and select the chunky/unblended setting.
- Serve and enjoy!

CARROT AND CORIANDER SOUP

INGREDIENTS

1x medium onion, chopped
6x medium carrots, chopped
2x medium potatoes, chopped
1x tsp dried coriander
2x vegetable stock cubes
1x bunch fresh coriander, chopped
Boiling water

INSTRUCTIONS

- Add all the ingredients **apart from the fresh coriander** to your soup maker.
- Add boiling water to top up your soup maker, ensure you do not go above the MAXIMUM or below the MINIMUM line.
- Put the lid on and select the smooth setting.
- At the end of the program, add the fresh coriander to the soup, optionally use the blend setting to make a completely smooth soup
- Serve and enjoy!

POTATO AND LEEK SOUP (CREAM OF)

INGREDIENTS

5x medium potatoes, chopped
2x leeks, chopped
2x vegetable stock cube
100ml double cream
Salt and pepper to taste
Sprig of parsley
Boiling water

INSTRUCTIONS

- Add all the ingredients **apart from the parsley** to your soup maker.
- Add boiling water to top up your soup maker, ensure you do not go above the MAXIMUM or below the MINIMUM line.
- Put the lid on and select the smooth setting.
- Add a sprig of parsley to each bowl
- Serve and enjoy!

POTATO AND BLUE CHEESE SOUP

INGREDIENTS

6x medium potatoes, chopped
2x medium onions, chopped
2x vegetable stock cubes
200g of Stilton (or alternative blue cheese)
Ground black pepper
Boiling water
Optional double cream

INSTRUCTIONS

- Add all of the ingredients **apart from the Stilton** to your soup maker.
- Add boiling water to top up your soup maker, ensure you do not go above the MAXIMUM or below the MINIMUM line.
- Put the lid on and select the smooth setting.
- When the program has finished, break the Stilton into smaller pieces and add to the soup maker, use the blend setting to reach desired consistency.
- Serve and enjoy!

Why not try adding 1 tbsp of double cream to each serving to compliment the blue cheese!

ONION SOUP

INGREDIENTS

8x medium onions, chopped
20g butter, salted
1x tbsp olive oil
1x tbsp plain flour
Salt and pepper to taste
Boiling water

INSTRUCTIONS

- Add all the ingredients to your soup maker.
- Add boiling water to top up your soup maker, ensure you do not go above the MAXIMUM or below the MINIMUM line.
- Put the lid on and select the smooth setting.
- Serve and enjoy!

MUSHROOM AND GARLIC SOUP

INGREDIENTS

3x medium onions, chopped
400g mushrooms, any variety, chopped
4x medium potatoes, chopped
20g butter, salted
4x garlic cloves, crushed and chopped
Salt and pepper to taste
Boiling water
Optional creme fraiche

INSTRUCTIONS

- Add all the ingredients **apart from the creme fraiche if using** to your soup maker.
- Add boiling water to top up your soup maker, ensure you do not go above the MAXIMUM or below the MINIMUM line.
- Put the lid on and select the smooth setting.
- Serve and enjoy!

Why not try adding a spoon of creme fraiche to your bowl of mushroom and garlic soup for an extra kick!

AJO BLANCO (GARLIC AND ALMOND SOUP)

INGREDIENTS

400g blanched almonds
75ml olive oil
3x garlic cloves, chopped
2x tbsp red wine (or red wine vinegar)
1x tsp salt
Cold water

INSTRUCTIONS

- Add all the ingredients to your soup maker.
- Add cold water to top up your soup maker to the MINIMUM line.
- Put the lid on and select the blend setting until the soup has a smooth consistency.
- Allow to cool in the fridge for up to 1 hour, serve chilled with a dusting of black pepper and a dash of olive oil for a tasty starter!

RED LENTIL SOUP

INGREDIENTS

200g red lentils, rinse and soak in a jug of water for approximately 60 minutes before use
1x medium onion, chopped
2x medium potatoes, chopped
2x vegetable stock cubes
Salt and pepper to taste
Boiling water

INSTRUCTIONS

- Add all of the ingredients to your soup maker.
- Add boiling water to top up your soup maker, ensure you do not go above the MAXIMUM or below the MINIMUM line.
- Put the lid on and select the smooth setting.
- Serve and enjoy!

Why not try a heartier soup by adding and extra 50g of red lentils and using the 'chunky' setting!

BEETROOT AND ORANGE SOUP

INGREDIENTS

600g cooked beetroot, chopped
200ml orange juice
1x medium onion, chopped
2x medium carrots, chopped
2x vegetable stock cubes
Salt and pepper to taste
Boiling water

INSTRUCTIONS

- Add all of the ingredients **apart from the orange juice** to your soup maker.
- Add boiling water to top up your soup maker, ensure you do not go above the MAXIMUM or below the MINIMUM line.
- Put the lid on and select the smooth setting.
- When the program is complete, allow to cool slightly and add the orange juice and mix well.
- Serve and enjoy!

SWEET POTATO AND BUTTERNUT SQUASH SOUP

INGREDIENTS

2x large sweet potatoes, chopped
1x large butternut squash, chopped
2x vegetable stock cubes
Salt and pepper to taste
Boiling water
Optional parsley and lemon juice for seasoning

INSTRUCTIONS

- Add all of the ingredients to your soup maker.
- Add boiling water to top up your soup maker, ensure you do not go above the MAXIMUM or below the MINIMUM line.
- Put the lid on and select the smooth setting.
- Serve and enjoy!

Why not try combining 3 tbsp lemon juice and some chopped parsley to create a delicious seasoning to add before serving!

Recipe Adjustments:

Printed in Great Britain
by Amazon